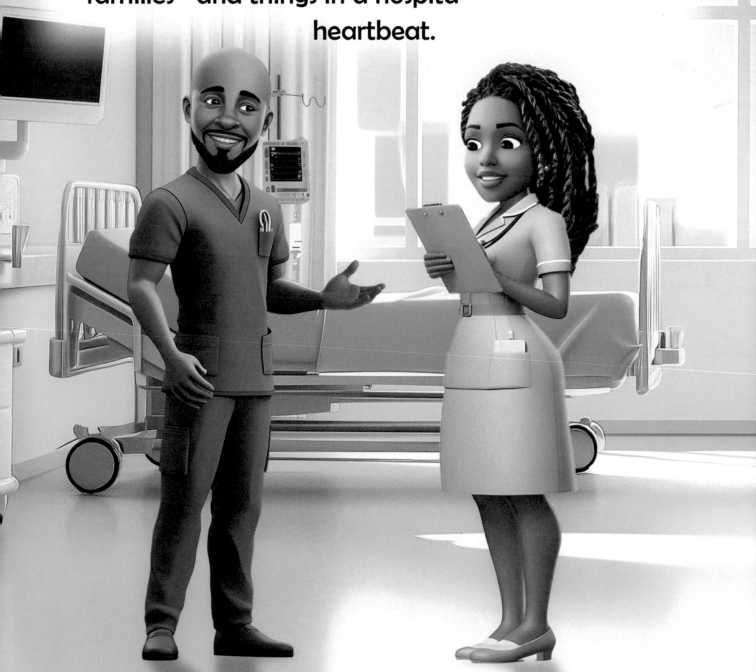

Nurses in the hospital care for p families—and things in a hospita heartbeat.

Aaliyah and her friend Quentin worked together as nurses on a surgery unit.

Aaliyah and Akiem enjoy doing so many things together. They like to go out to eat and work out at the fitness center together.

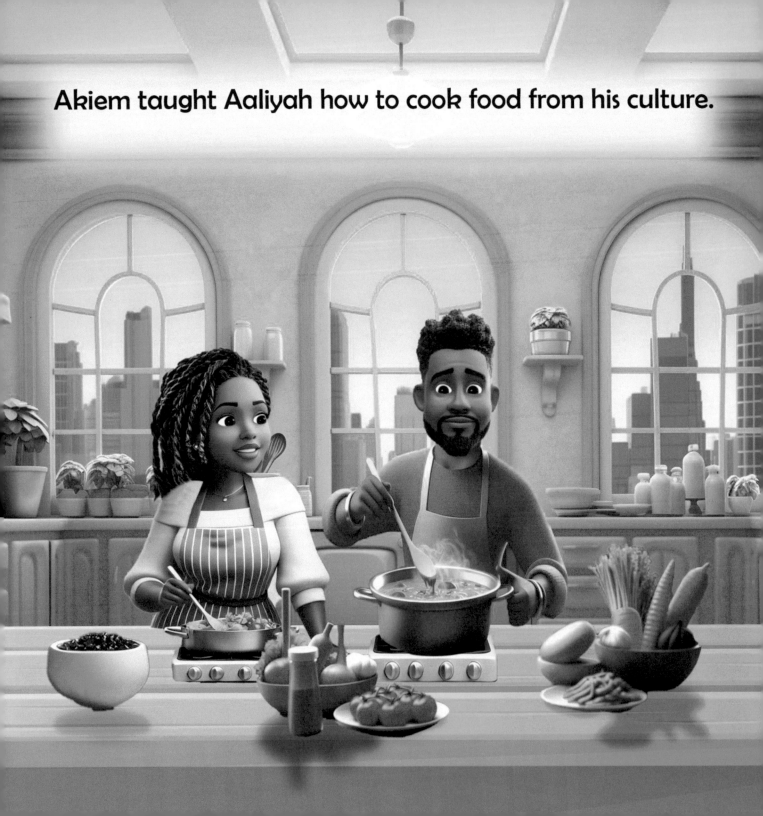

Akiem taught Aaliyah how to cook food from his culture.

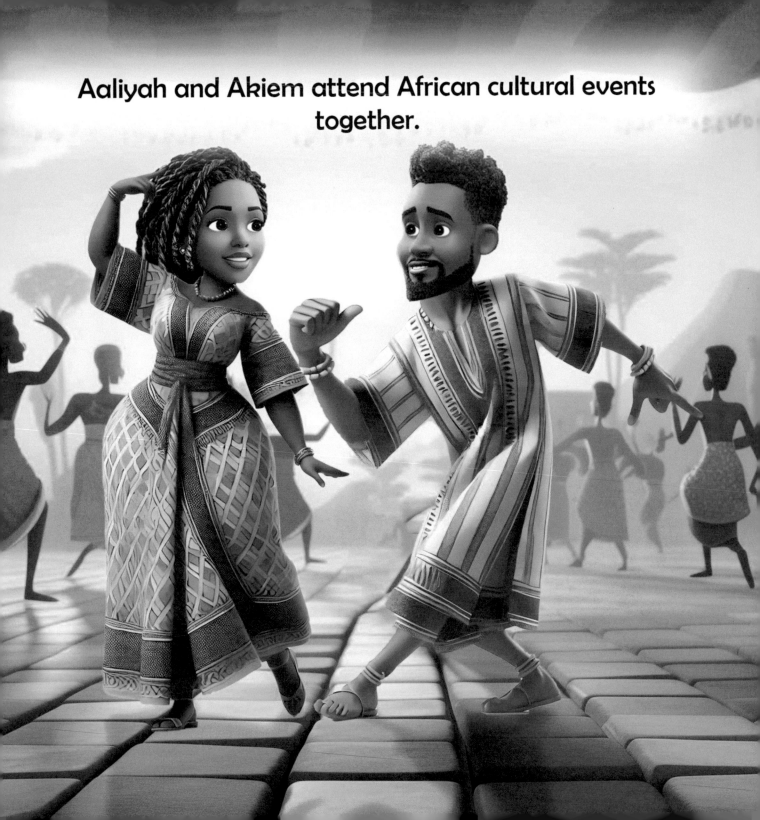

Aaliyah and Akiem attend African cultural events together.

Aaliyah and Akiem spend time with her family. Akiem loves talking with Aaliyah's mom.

Aaliyah and Akiem pray together as a family.

On their first Christmas together, Aaliyah and Akiem put up decorations in their new home.

Made in the USA
Columbia, SC
05 January 2025

51310448R00018